# Why Do Ice Cubes Float?

Thomas Canavan

**W**

FRANKLIN WATTS

LONDON • SYDNEY

First published in 2013 by Franklin Watts

Copyright © 2013 Arcturus Publishing Limited

Franklin Watts
338 Euston Road
London
NW1 3BH

Franklin Watts Australia
Level 17/207 Kent Street, Sydney, NSW 2000

Produced by Arcturus Publishing Limited,
26/27 Bickels Yard, 151–153 Bermondsey Street, London SE1 3HA

Editor: Joe Harris
Picture researcher: Joe Harris
Designer: Ian Winton

Picture credits: All images supplied by Shutterstock except bottom image page 14: Sally Henry and Trevor Cook.

A CIP catalogue record for this book is available from the British Library.

Dewey Decimal Classification Number: 620.1'12

ISBN: 978 1 4451 2238 0

Franklin Watts is a division of Hachette Children's Books, an Hachette UK company.
www.hachette.co.uk

Printed in China

SL002663EN
Supplier 03, Date 0513 Print Run 2365

# Contents

TOP SECRET

# Food for thought

Cooking is really just a type of science – except you get to eat the results of your experiments. It's time to put on your white lab coat, or is that an apron?

## Why does popcorn **pop**?

A popcorn kernel has an outer case with a starchy inside. There's usually a little water inside too. When the kernel is heated enough the water boils. The boiling water becomes a gas and suddenly expands. This 'pops' the outer case and turns the kernel inside out. The yummy white fluffy bits are the starch.

## How does yeast make bread rise?

Yeast is a type of fungus that becomes active when it is warmed. Bakers mix it into bread dough. Then they leave it somewhere warm. The yeast begins to feed on the sugar in the dough. As it does, it gives off a gas that puffs up the dough.

4

# How do sweet-makers get the words into seaside rock?

Rock is made by boiling sugar until it looks like white modelling clay. As it cools it is stretched into long strips. Some bits are coloured and pulled out into long string shapes. The clever part is arranging the coloured strings along the white strips to make words when the whole thing is rolled up. The thick roll is then stretched until it turns into a long, thin piece of rock.

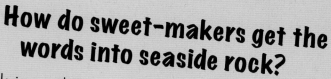

SCIENCE
FAQ

FAQ
SCIENCE

FAQ
SCIENCE

# Why do stale biscuits get soggy but stale bread goes dry?

Biscuits start off dry and have less water than the air around them. Bread and cake have a little more water than the air around them. The water moves from where there's more to where there's less. That means it goes from the air into the biscuits – making them soggy. And it goes from the bread into the air – making it drier.

5

# Now for some hard questions

Let's hope your brain can cope with these hard questions. Or should that be, questions about hardness? This sort of science isn't for softies – that's for sure!

## What is the hardest rock?

Diamond is the hardest thing that we can find in the ground. But scientists tell us that diamond is a mineral. A rock is something that's made of two or more minerals. Several types of rock compete for the title of 'hardest'. Most of them, like sandstone and quartzite, contain the mineral quartz.

## Why don't we use solid tyres for cars and bikes any more?

Well, we'd never worry about punctures. But solid tyres would be heavy and they wouldn't be as good at softening the blow when we hit bumps. Another problem is that hard, smooth tyres would make cars and bikes difficult to control.

## Is there really such a thing as bullet-proof glass?

Yes, and it stops most bullets. The 'glass' is really a sandwich of three layers. The outer and inner layers are made of normal windscreen glass. Between them is a layer of strong, clear plastic. A bullet smashes the outer layer but the plastic soaks up its force.

## What metal did knights use for their armour?

Most suits of armour were made of iron or steel. The earliest looked like long dressing gowns. They were made of small rings of iron, called chainmail. Later on, knights wore suits made from flat pieces of metal, called plates. These plates connected to make a suit.

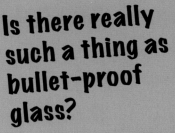

# It's only natural

Here are a few FAQs to take you 'back to nature'. Did you have any idea that there was so much science going on all around you in the natural world?

## Why is there often a special smell just before it rains?

The smell is from a gas called ozone. High up in the atmosphere, a layer of ozone protects Earth from harmful radiation. But the electricity in lightning can produce ozone nearer the ground. The ozone spreads out from rain clouds, and often reaches you before the rain arrives.

## Why do plants grow better in some soils than in others?

Just like animals, plants need to take in food to grow and stay healthy. Minerals and other natural 'plant foods' are called nutrients. Some soils have more nutrients than others, and some soils suit certain plants more than others.

# Could someone squeeze a piece of coal and turn it into diamond, like Superman?

Superman may have been able to do that trick, but it would never happen in nature. Both coal and diamond are made from a mineral called carbon. But they are quite different. Coal started out as plants. Over millions of years the dead plants were squished into coal. Diamonds formed even longer ago, at very high temperatures deep inside the Earth.

# How do solar panels turn sunlight into electricity?

Both sunlight and electricity are made up of tiny objects called particles. The particles in sunlight are called photons. Electricity is a movement of particles called electrons. When photons of sunlight hit the silicon in a solar panel, they knock electrons off the silicon. Those electrons become an electric current.

# It all boils down to science

Boiling, melting and freezing. You come across these science events every time you boil a kettle, lick a lolly or go skating on an ice rink. Give these questions some real thought, but don't get too steamed up!

## Why do we sprinkle salt on icy roads?

It's all down to the freezing temperature of water. Normally that's 0°C (32°F). But salt water freezes at a lower temperature. That means that salt water stays liquid at 0°C (32°F). So the salt we sprinkle on roads and paths prevents water from turning into ice so easily.

## Why do some kettles whistle?

The spout has a lid with two pieces of metal inside it. They're about 3 mm (1/8 in) apart. Each of them has a small hole in the middle. High-pressure steam from the kettle's boiling water rushes through these holes. It swirls around the narrow gap between the bits of metal. The swirling makes the whistling sound as the steam passes through the holes.

# How do igloos stay warm without melting?

Igloos are good insulators. That means they keep cold air out and warmer air in. The blocks are made of hard snow. Even hard snow contains air – and it's trapped air that does the insulation work. The inside does melt just a little when people are in the igloo. But it freezes again when they're gone.

# Why can you 'see your breath' in the winter?

Your breath contains water – not liquid water, but water as a gas. In the winter, your breath cools down suddenly as it leaves your warm body. The water changes from being a gas into being thousands of tiny drops of moisture. Those drops look like fog.

11

# Pass the gas

You will probably breathe in and out more than 600 million times in your life. Yet how much do you know about the air that you breathe? Or the other gases that are all around you?

## Which gas makes people's voices sound funny?

The gas is helium. It's the same gas that's inside floating balloons. Helium is less dense than normal air. It travels through your throat faster when you talk. That extra speed changes the way your voice sounds.

## Why are packets of crisps filled with air?

Crisp packets are pumped full of gas before they're sealed. That's to protect the crisps from getting broken. But the gas isn't air. It's nitrogen. Air contains oxygen, which makes crisps go stale. Nitrogen doesn't do that, and it doesn't affect the taste of the crisps.

## Why do fizzy drinks fizz?

The bubbles in fizzy drinks are carbon dioxide. This gas is added to the drink before the bottle or can is sealed. The carbon dioxide is under a lot of pressure (it is pushed from all directions). This keeps the carbon dioxide dissolved in the drink. When you open the can, there is suddenly less pressure. The carbon dioxide rushes to become a gas again – by fizzing up.

## Why do some balloons float but others don't?

A balloon will float if it's full of a gas that's lighter than air. Helium is the most common light gas for filling toy balloons because it is safe. A balloon filled with normal air will fall slowly to the ground because of the weight of the balloon.

# Read all about it

You don't need to be reading a science textbook to learn about science. Just take a closer look at the paper, ink, pencils and rubbers that you use every day.

## How does invisible ink work?

A simple method uses heat to unlock a secret message. Dip a stick in milk or lemon juice and write your message. Let it dry and become invisible. Then hold a hair dryer up to the paper. The letters will appear! That's because the heat has caused acids in the dried 'ink' to change colour.

TOP SECRET

## Can you stick two books together without using glue?

Yes, and the secret comes from the force of friction. Face the open pages of two paperback books at each other. Slowly fan the pages so that the pages of each book extend about 5 cm (2 in) into the other. Now try to pull them apart. It's hard because the force of friction builds up with each overlap.

# Why does old paper turn yellow?

Paper is made of wood. The part of wood called cellulose makes paper white. But wood also contains a dark substance called lignin. This adds strength to wood. Over time the lignin in paper breaks down and forms yellow-coloured acids. And it's these that turn the paper yellow.

# How do pencil erasers work?

A pencil line is actually a string of tiny flakes of graphite across the surface of paper. Graphite is the dark material at the point of a sharp pencil. An eraser scrubs the paper's surface. That removes the bits of graphite as well as a little of the paper itself. It also uses up some of the eraser's rubber.

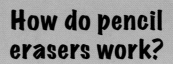

# Whatever floats your boat

Some of the most interesting science facts are all about staying afloat or staying up in the air. It's sink or swim, so hang on in there and check out these answers.

## How do huge ships float?

A huge object pushes away lots of water. If it's heavier than the water it pushes away, it will sink. If it's lighter than that water, it will float. A big ship is heavy, but not as heavy as that much water. It has lots of empty spaces that are full of air.

## Does all wood float?

Most wood floats because there's lots of air inside between the wood cells. That makes wood weigh less than water – and float. Some types of wood, such as ebony, are very dense. That means their wood cells are packed so tightly there's not much room for air. These woods will sink in water.

16

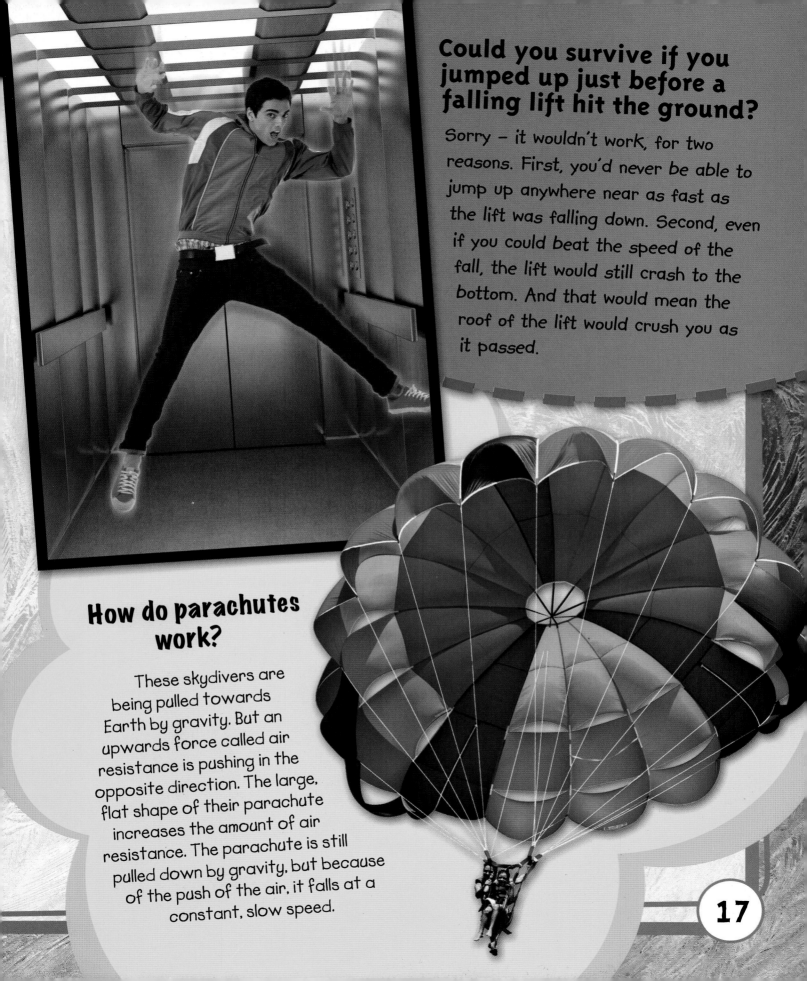

## Could you survive if you jumped up just before a falling lift hit the ground?

Sorry – it wouldn't work, for two reasons. First, you'd never be able to jump up anywhere near as fast as the lift was falling down. Second, even if you could beat the speed of the fall, the lift would still crash to the bottom. And that would mean the roof of the lift would crush you as it passed.

## How do parachutes work?

These skydivers are being pulled towards Earth by gravity. But an upwards force called air resistance is pushing in the opposite direction. The large, flat shape of their parachute increases the amount of air resistance. The parachute is still pulled down by gravity, but because of the push of the air, it falls at a constant, slow speed.

17

# Water wonders

Jump in and make a big splash with these questions about the way water behaves. Is it playing tricks on us, or can we get to the bottom of these FAQs?

## Why do ice cubes float?

It's a good question. Most substances are more dense in their solid form. This means they sink in liquid. But water is unusual. It is less dense in its solid form – ice – than in its liquid form – water. So that's why ice cubes float in water.

## How can some insects walk across water?

Water molecules are attracted to other molecules on all sides. But those on the surface have none above them. This makes them hold on to their other neighbours more strongly. And that hold creates a delicate film which can support light objects without breaking. Scientists call it surface tension.

18

# Why do clothes dry on a washing line even when the Sun isn't out?

Because the water in the wet clothes evaporates. The molecules in a liquid are constantly crashing into each other. They pass energy along with each crash. Some molecules wind up with enough energy to break free of the liquid and become a gas. This is evaporation - and it's how your clothes get dry.

# Why are soap bubbles round?

Even if you blow a bubble through a square wand, the bubble is still round. Weird, huh? It happens like this. When you blow through the wand, the bubble forms with air inside. The shape that uses the least energy to form is a sphere (a round shape). So even if it starts off as a long sausage shape while you blow, your bubble will always end up round.

19

# Are you stuck?

Here's the crazy place where science becomes magic. Or is it the other way round? It's time to stick together as we enter the world of stick and non-stick.

## How does Velcro work?

Velcro is simple. It has two pieces. One has lots and lots of small plastic hooks. The other piece has loads of tiny loops made of string. The hooks fit into the loops when the pieces go together. Velcro is strong because there are so many locking hooks and loops.

## How do non-stick pans work?

Here's an example of chemistry helping you out in everyday life. The non-stick part of the pan is a layer of Teflon. That brand name is easier to say than the official chemical name of this substance – polytetrafluoroethylene. Teflon does not react with other substances, which means that things don't stick to it.

## Why do magnets pick up some things and not others?

Magnets can only affect other magnets. What makes something magnetic? Inside any substance, you will find tiny specks of matter called electrons. In a magnetic substance, such as iron, some of those electrons aren't linked to any other electrons. These electrons can line up to form loads of 'mini magnets'. But in non-magnetic substances, all the electrons are linked to each other. They cancel out each other's possible magnetic force.

## How does glue make things stick together?

Scientists can't agree on the whole explanation! They know that most glues start off as liquids and finish as solids. To work well they need to seep into dips and ridges on the things they're attaching. Once they've become solids, the two things are held together. But scientists will have to look more and more closely – down to the tiny level of atoms and beyond – to work out why the glue really sticks.

# That's really cool!

What turns up the heat and how do you stay cool? Check out these hot and cold questions to find out.

## How do fans make you feel cooler?

They do that because of evaporation. Liquids, including your sweat, evaporate more quickly in a breeze. That's why clothes dry better on a windy day. Heat is given off when liquid evaporates. And that makes you feel cooler.

## Why does metal feel colder to touch than wood or plastic?

Metal conducts heat much better than wood or plastic. That means it takes away more of your body heat when you touch it. And that makes it feel colder than touching the wood or plastic.

# How much heat do hats really hold in?

Grown-ups are always telling children to wear hats on cold days to keep warm. But how much heat actually escapes upwards? Scientists have shown that you lose about 10 per cent of body heat through your head. And that's because your head takes up about 10 per cent of your body surface.

## Why do woollen clothes shrink in a dryer?

Wool fibres have lots of small scales on their surface. They look like tiny roof shingles. These scales lift up when wool is exposed to heat and damp - exactly what you find in a dryer. The fibres rub together and the scales lock into each other. This pulls the wool in tighter, making it shrink.

# Metal workout

Metals are tough and last for ever. Right?
What would you think if you found out that
a lot of metals are just softies at heart?

## Can stainless steel rust?

Steel is a mixture of iron and carbon. It is
strong but it rusts in much the same way
as iron itself. If you add chromium, you
produce stainless steel. Chromium gives
stainless steel its shine. It also provides a
barrier to stop oxygen getting at the steel.
Without oxygen, the chemical reaction that
produces rust cannot take place.

## Why does a coat hanger break if you bend it back and forth?

It's all because of something called metal fatigue. Fatigue means
'tiredness', and that's a good description of what happens. Bending the
metal back and forth opens up tiny cracks in the surface of the metal.
The cracks get wider and wider until... the hanger breaks.

# Why does oil make tools last longer?

The metal bits of tools look smooth, but their edges are uneven. When they move against each other, these uneven bits catch. The tool doesn't work so well and the moving bits wear down. Oil keeps those bits from touching each other. They can still move back and forth, but they don't catch any more.

# Why does a razor blade go blunt if it only has to cut hair?

You'd have to look closely – really closely – at the blade to find out. A human hair is harder to cut than copper wire of the same size. It knocks atoms off the edge of the blade when the razor hits it. Lots of hairs knock lots of atoms off. And without the straight line of atoms forming an edge, the blade gets dull and blunt.

25

# Changing things

Science is full of things that change from one thing to another, things that change shape, or things that do unusual things. Okay, that's enough things! Let's have a look at the science...

## What is smoke?

Smoke is all the bits that aren't burned up in a fire. Only water and carbon dioxide are left behind when things are completely burned. But a fire can't burn everything if it doesn't have enough oxygen or if it hasn't become hot enough. So smoke is a mixture of tiny bits of solid, liquid and gas that are all the leftovers, floating in the air.

## What happens when paper is recycled?

Paper is made from wood pulp (wood that's mushed up). The first step at a recycling centre is to add water to the old paper. That makes it easy to mush up and become pulp again. Then the pulp goes through a screen to get rid of ink, glue and other bits of material. It's then ready to become paper again.

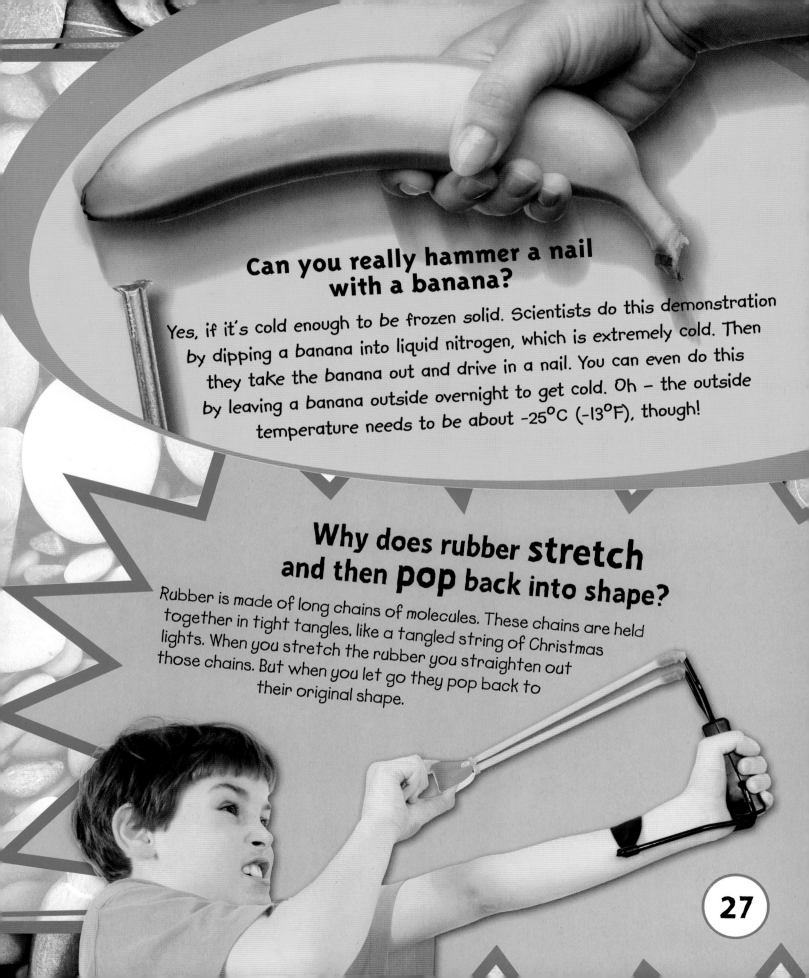

## Can you really hammer a nail with a banana?

Yes, if it's cold enough to be frozen solid. Scientists do this demonstration by dipping a banana into liquid nitrogen, which is extremely cold. Then they take the banana out and drive in a nail. You can even do this by leaving a banana outside overnight to get cold. Oh – the outside temperature needs to be about -25°C (-13°F), though!

## Why does rubber stretch and then pop back into shape?

Rubber is made of long chains of molecules. These chains are held together in tight tangles, like a tangled string of Christmas lights. When you stretch the rubber you straighten out those chains. But when you let go they pop back to their original shape.

27

# Still stumped?

Did you really think that you'd come to the end of the line and there were no more questions to answer? Wrong! The world around you is full of science FAQs. Here are a few to keep you thinking.

## How do duvets keep us so warm?

They work because air is a good insulator. That means that it doesn't let heat pass through it easily. The feathers fluff up the duvet so that it's mainly air inside its cover. The duvet doesn't actually warm you. Instead it keeps your own heat inside it and near you.

## Is anywhere in the world hot enough to fry an egg on the pavement?

Not quite, if you think of putting the frying pan on its own on the pavement. Nowhere on Earth has reached 70°C (158°F), the temperature when an egg begins to fry. But it could work on a really hot day if you put the pan in a glass-topped box with foil walls. That would concentrate the sun's heat.

# Why do golf balls bounce so high?

The inside of a golf ball is made from materials that compress (change shape when pressed) a lot. That means they can absorb a lot of energy when a club hits them or if they land on a hard surface. But that same material immediately tries to get back to its round shape. It's that 'fighting back' that gives the ball its bounce.

# Why is it easier to wrinkle clothes than to iron them?

Wrinkles are just folds. And those folds are all straight lines. The fibres (tiny strands) in clothes like to line up in lines. Plus they like to stay lined up. That's why it's easy to wrinkle clothes and harder to 'unwrinkle' them. Wetting the clothes before ironing helps to relax the fibres. That makes ironing a little easier.

# Glossary

**absorb** To take in from outside.

**acid** A chemical substance that often has a sour or sharp taste, such as vinegar.

**air resistance** A force that acts against objects moving through the air.

**atom** The basic building block of all matter.

**cellulose** A complicated chemical sugar that is a basic ingredient of plants.

**dense** Having a lot of weight in a small area.

**electric current** A flow of electrons carrying electrical energy.

**electron** A negatively charged particle that is part of an atom.

**energy** The scientific name given to the ability to do work.

**evaporate** To change from a liquid to a gas.

**fibre** A narrow string-like piece of material that makes up something larger.

**film** A thin covering.

**force** A push or pull on an object because it meets another object.

**friction** A force produced when one object is moved along another.

**fungus** A group of living things that often look like plants but which cannot produce their own food.

**gravity** The force that pulls objects in space towards each other. On Earth, gravity pulls them towards the centre of the planet.

**insulator** Something that prevents the flow of heat or other forms of energy.

**invisible** Not able to be seen.

**lignin** The tough, fibrous part of wood and plants — the substance that makes vegetables firm and crunchy.

**mineral** A substance found naturally in the ground.

**moisture** Wetness.

**molecule** The smallest unit of a substance, made up of a group of atoms. For example, a water molecule is made up of two atoms of hydrogen and one atom of oxygen.

**nutrient** Something that provides food for plants or animals.

**photon** A tiny particle of light energy.

**pressure** The force of pushing on something.

**radiation** The process of sending off waves of energy.

**react** To change because of coming into contact with something else.

**silicon** An element that is very common on Earth — it is found in sand and in quartz.

**starch** A mixture of chemical sugars found in plants.

# Further Reading

*Belair on Display — Hands on Science* by Carolyn Dale (Collins Educational, 2011)

*Explore* by Sean Callery, Clive Gifford and Dr Mike Goldsmith (Kingfisher, 2008)

*Material World: The Science of Big Bang Science Experiments* by Jay Hawkins (Windmill Books, 2013)

*Metal (Everyday Materials)* by Andrew Langley (Wayland Books, 2008)

*Science Made Easy: Materials and Their Properties* by Carol Vorderman (Dorling Kindersley, 2011)

*Using Water (The Green Team)* by Sally Hewitt (Franklin Watts, 2011)

# Websites

**BBC — KS2 Bitesize**
**www.bbc.co.uk/bitesize/ks2/science/materials/**
The BBC's widely respected Bitesize website has an excellent section devoted to Materials Science.

**Penn State Food Science for Kids**
**http://foodscience.psu.edu/youth**
The famous university's College of Agricultural Sciences has created an enticing introduction to Food Science.

**Science Buddies**
**www.sciencebuddies.org/science -fair-projects/science-engineering-careers/MatlSci_materialsscientistsandengineers_coo1.shtml**

This is the place to come if you're interested in what it takes to become a materials scientist...and in all the fascinating ways that materials scientists widen our knowledge.

**Science Kids**
**www.sciencekids.co.nz/metals.html**
The lively and innovative New Zealand website uses an introduction to metals as a portal into a wide-ranging journey through the world of material sciences.

**Strange Matter**
**www.strangematterexhibit.com/**
'Discover the secrets of everyday stuff', the home page promises, before leading you through a hair-raising tour of materials science in all its guises.

# Index

# Series contents

**Do Plants Really Eat Insects?** • It's a jungle out there! • Try this for size • Peckish plants • Jobs to do • Birds and bees... and trees • Peculiar plants • Changing nature • Going to extremes • Get a life! • Power plants • Eat your greens! • Don't be so wet! • Just wondering

**Does It Really Rain Frogs?** • Home sweet globe • Stormy weather • Round and round • The right impression • A large shake, please • Forcing the issue • Just give me some time • Lighten up • Making a splash • Rain, rain, go away • Now you've done it • Going to extremes • Air we go

**What Makes You Hiccup?** • It's break time • I beg your pardon • Act your age • Just be sensible • Pick up the pace • Pass it on • Eye eye, sir • Food for thought • Sleep secrets • Hair, there and everywhere • Skin deep • I don't feel well • Anybody's guess

**Why Are Black Holes Black?** • Sunny side up • Meet the neighbours • Hey — lighten up! • Over the moon • Up, up and away • Here comes trouble • Sky-high science • Goin' my way? • Tighten your space helmet • Heavens above • Long ago and far away... • That's life! • It's out of this world

**Why Do Ice Cubes Float?** • Food for thought • Now for some hard questions • It's only natural • It all boils down to science • Pass the gas • Read all about it • Whatever floats your boat • Water wonders • Are you stuck? • That's really cool! • Metal workout • Changing things • Still stumped?

**Why Do Zebras Have Stripes?** • Going for the record • What you see is what you get • All at sea? • Come to your senses • Jurassic park life • Creepy crawlies • Yackety-yak • Baby beasties • What's for dinner? • Up and away • Fact or fiction? • Just like us? • It's round-up time